Animals of the Night

BIG CATS
AFTER DARK

Ruth O'Shaughnessy

Enslow Publishing
101 W. 23rd Street
Suite 240
New York, NY 10011
USA

enslow.com

Words to Know

camouflage—An animal's coloring that helps it blend with its habitat.

carnivore—An animal that eats meat.

extinct—To have died out; a type of animal becomes extinct when all of its members die.

habitat—The place in which an animal lives.

mammal—An animal that has a backbone, hair, usually gives birth to live babies, and produces milk to feed its young.

prey—An animal hunted by another animal for food.

pride—A group of lions that live together.

prowl—To move about quietly and secretly.

savanna—A grassy plain.

stalk—To watch and follow prey from a distance.

Contents

On the Prowl in Russia

Night falls in the snow-covered, birch forests of Russia. A hungry Siberian tiger **prowls** through the trees, slowly and silently, hidden from an unsuspecting herd of elk. The large cat is on the hunt.

The tiger fixes its gaze on a young elk that has become separated from the herd. The stealthy cat quietly creeps up on it and waits behind some bushes. Then it pounces! The elk has no chance of escape. The tiger holds it down with its razor-sharp claws and clamps its jaws around the elk's throat, biting down until the elk dies. This powerful hunter has found its meal.

A Siberian tiger
hunts for food.

The Fierce Four

The tiger is a big cat. The phrase "big cat" has different meanings, but scientists often use it to describe cats that roar. Only four cats do that—lions, tigers, leopards, and jaguars. This group of animals is called *Panthera*.

Besides the ability to roar, big cats have other things in common. All big cats are very large. A male lion can be about 9 feet (3 meters) long from head to tail. The largest of the big cats, the Siberian tiger, can weigh more than 600 pounds (272 kilograms)!

A big cat's strong, muscular body allows it to run fast and jump high. Its long tail helps it keep its balance. Most big cats are great climbers and swimmers.

A male lion goes after prey.
A lion can run 37 miles
(59 kilometers) per hour.

Yet big cats are not always on the move. They spend quite a bit of time napping. The African lion spends up to twenty hours a day sleeping or resting. Hunting takes a lot of energy, so they usually rest during the day and become active at night.

Big cats belong to a group of mammals called carnivores. Carnivores have special teeth for cutting meat. Their four long, pointed front teeth are called canines. These help to hold their prey. Other teeth toward the back, called carnassials (kar-nas-ee-als), tear off chunks of meat. Big cats also have powerful jaws and razor-sharp claws.

Fun Fact!

Big cats' brains are large for their body size, so they are very smart. They know the distance between them and other animals, which helps in hunting.

A lioness, or female lion, naps in a tree. She must build up her energy during the day to hunt at night.

Coats That Camouflage

Each of the big cats has a different coat. The color and pattern on its fur lets the animal blend in well with its surroundings. This is known as camouflage. A tiger's stripes are hard to see in the forest's shadows. The lion's tan fur matches the tan, dried grass in African grasslands. The spots on the coats of leopards and jaguars are called rosettes. Leopards often watch for their prey in trees. Their spotted coats blend with the leaves, making them hard to see. Some leopards and jaguars are born with black coats. This makes them very hard to see after dark, which helps in night hunting.

Fun Fact!

A leopard's spots and a tiger's stripes are like a person's fingerprints. No two leopards or tigers have exactly the same pattern.

These two leopards may look the same, but each cat's coat pattern is unique.

Big Cat Habitats

Although the lion is called the "king of the jungle," most lions are found on the grassy plains of Africa called savannas. They also live in open woodlands. But a small number of lions can be found in the Gir Forest of India. Leopards live in forests, grasslands, mountains, and deserts in Africa and Asia.

Tigers are only found in Asia. However, these animals can live in lots of different places. There are tigers in the freezing cold areas of Siberia as well as in hot rain forests.

Jaguars are the only big cats in the Americas. They mostly live near water in rain forests and swampy grasslands.

A jaguar stretches after a nap. Jaguars are found in Central and South America.

Most big cats are lone hunters. Only lions live in groups called **prides**. A pride may have up to three males, about a dozen females, and their cubs, or babies. The females are all related. All cats mark the area they live in. They do this by scratching trees to leave their scent. They also urinate or leave their droppings.

Big cats often roar to warn other cats to stay away. Some nights, a whole pride of lions may roar. A lion's roar can be heard for miles. Big cats also grunt, hiss, growl, and snarl.

Fun Fact!

A tiger also makes a noise called a chuffle, which almost sounds like a sneeze. It is a friendly greeting similar to a house cat's purr.

females do the hunting.

Amazing Senses

Big cats are nocturnal, which means they are active mostly at night. These animals see well in the dark. They have a feature in the back of their eyes that reflect light, making their eyes glow. A tiger can see six times better than a human can at night. Big cats can also hear sounds that humans cannot. They can turn their ears toward a sound and tell where it is coming from. This can be quite useful when hunting after dark.

A big cat's whiskers help at night too. Whiskers act as "feelers." They help a cat tell if something is close by in the dark.

Fun Fact!

Like house cats, big cats spend a lot of time grooming themselves with their rough, spiky tongues. The tiny spikes act like a comb, pulling out dirt along with any loose hairs.

Tiger eyes see much better in darkness than human eyes.

Top Predators

Big cats are top predators, which means they are at the top of the food chain. They kill other animals for food but are not hunted themselves. Some **stalk** their prey—they quietly follow their victim from a distance. Others wait in hiding for an animal. Then they jump on their prey. They quickly pull it to the ground.

Lions, leopards, and tigers usually bite the animal's throat. This crushes its neck so it cannot breathe. Jaguars most often bite their prey's skull to kill it.

Leopard teeth are sharp and strong enough to crush an animal's throat.

Big cats often drag their dead prey to a private spot. They eat as much as they can and then bury what's left under leaves and dirt to save for later. Leopards and jaguars are very strong and sometimes drag their victims, which are often much heavier then they are, up a tree. There they can enjoy their meal without other animals trying to steal their food.

Fun Fact!

A tiger can eat about 40 pounds (18 kilograms) of meat in a meal.

A leopard drags her kill up a tree so other predators do not try to steal it. Her cub eats its meal in peace.

Surviving in the Wild

As top predators, big cats have no natural enemies. However, when a new male lion takes over a pride, he will kill the cubs of the old male. He then mates with the females and they have his cubs.

Tigers do not live in groups. But male tigers will also sometimes kill the cubs of other males. Then they mate with the female. Leopards have also been known to kill cubs that are not theirs when they take over an area.

Humans are the greatest danger to big cats. Hunting these cats is against the law in many places. However, these laws are not always obeyed.

A ranger, a person who protects wildlife reserves, examines lion bones in South Africa. More and more lions are being hunted by people who sell the bones to other countries.

Family Life

The mating behaviors of all the big cats are the same. The female gives off a special scent when she is ready to mate, which draws the male. Then she playfully rolls around on the ground to let the male know that she wants to mate.

A few months after mating, the female gives birth to cubs, which are helpless at birth. They drink their mother's milk for their first few months. During this time, their mother also protects them from larger animals that may want to eat them.

Usually two to three cubs are born. But sometimes there may be as many as five or six. As the cubs get older, they watch their mother hunt. During this time, the playful cubs practice stalking small birds and insects. After about two years, big cats begin to hunt alone and are ready to live on their own.

A lioness keeps a watchful eye over her two young cubs as they play-fight.

Relationship with People

The only creatures big cats have to fear are humans. Many big cats lose their habitats when people clear forests and jungles to make way for towns and farms. Sometimes big cats wander into areas where people live, looking for food. They are often killed.

Big cats are also killed for their beautiful fur. Leopard coats are expensive and very popular. Tigers are sometimes killed for their body parts because some people wrongly believe that a tiger's body parts can cure sicknesses. Big cats are also killed for sport. Both of these activities are usually against the law.

Authorities caught the criminals who tried to sell these tiger skins and leopard skins.

The killing by humans has shrunk the number of big cats in the wild. Some types of big cats, tigers especially, could become extinct. However, people are trying to save them.

Countries have passed laws that make it a crime to kill or harm these animals. They also have made the punishments harsher for lawbreakers.

Some zoos are helping by breeding big cats to increase their numbers, and teaching people about these magnificent animals. Some people hope to save large areas of these animals' habitats too. Caring people are working hard to make sure big cats are still around in the future.

This leopard cub is being weighed in a zoo in Germany. Breeding programs help big cat species survive.

Stay Safe Around Big Cats

Unless you travel to or live on the African plains, the jungles in Southeast Asia, or the rain forests of Central and South America, there is probably little chance of you running into a big cat. But there are people who do live in these areas, and many others who travel there. People have come up with ways to lower the risk of being attacked by these powerful predators. For example, because tigers do not like to attack from the front, jungle workers wear face masks on the backs of their heads. This makes a tiger always think the person is facing it. Here are a few other safety tips to follow:

- Do not go out at night when big cats are most active.

- Do not go out alone. Always have a group of two or more people with you.

- Keep pets and farm animals indoors at night.

- Although the cubs of big cats are very cute, they should never be taken as pets. Leave them alone and get away from the area. Their mother is probably nearby and would see you as a threat to her babies.

- Never feed a big cat or the animals it preys on.

- When face to face with a big cat, do not run. Running only makes it more likely to chase you. Scream to try to scare it.

Learn More

Books

Guillain, Charlotte. *Jaguars*. North Mankato, Minn.: Heinemann-Raintree, 2014.

Hirsch, Rebecca E. *Siberian Tigers: Camouflaged Hunting Mammals*. Minneapolis, Minn.: Lerner Publications, 2015.

Ringstad, Arnold. *Lions*. Mankato, Minn.: Black Rabbit Books, 2015.

Throp, Claire. *Leopards*. North Mankato, Minn.: Heinemann-Raintree, 2014.

Web Sites

animals.nationalgeographic.com/animals/big-cats/facts/

Learn facts about big cats.

animals.sandiegozoo.org/animals/tiger

Read about the six different kinds of tigers left in the world.

animals.sandiegozoo.org/animals/leopard

Discover what goes on in the life of a leopard.

Index

Published in 2016 by Enslow Publishing, LLC.
101 W. 23rd Street, Suite 240, New York, NY 10011

Copyright © 2016 by the estate of Elaine Landau
Enslow Publishing materials copyright © 2016 by Enslow Publishing, LLC.

Library of Congress Cataloging-in-Publication Data
O'Shaughnessy, Ruth, author.
 Big cats after dark / Ruth O'Shaughnessy.
   pages cm. — (Animals of the night)
 Summary: "Discusses big cats, their behavior, and environment"—Provided by publisher.
 Audience: Ages 8+
 Audience: Grades 4 to 6.
 Includes bibliographical references and index.
 ISBN 978-0-7660-7046-2 (library binding)
 ISBN 978-0-7660-7044-8 (pbk.)
 ISBN 978-0-7660-7045-5 (6-pack)
 1. Felidae—Juvenile literature. 2. Nocturnal animals—Juvenile literature. 3. Animal behavior—Juvenile literature. I. Title.
 QL737.C23O84 2016
 599.75—dc23
                            2015009970

Printed in the United States of America

To Our Readers: We have done our best to make sure all Web site addresses in this book were active and appropriate when we went to press. However, the author and the publisher have no control over and assume no liability for the material available on those Web sites or on any Web sites they may link to. Any comments or suggestions can be sent by e-mail to customerservice@enslow.com.

Portions of this book originally appeared in the book *Big Cats: Hunters of the Night*.

Photo Credits: Aditya Singh/Moment/Getty Images, p. 3; by toonman/Moment Open/Getty Images, p. 17; China Photos/Stringer/Getty Images, p. 27; David & Micha Sheldon/F1online/Getty Images, p. 5; Doug Cheeseman/Photolibrary/Getty Images, p. 9; Hoberman Collection/Universal Images Group/Getty Images, p. 21; Justin Lo/Moment Open/Getty Images, p. 13; kimberrywood/Digital Vision Vectors/Getty Images (green moon dingbat); Manoj Shah/The Image Bank/ Getty Images, p. 25; narvikk/E+/Getty Images (starry background); Odd Anderson/AFP/Getty Images, p. 29; Pavlo Burdyak/Shutterstock.com (lion), p. 1; Pete Walentin/Getty Images, p. 7; Picture by Tambako the Jaguar/Moment/ Getty Images, p. 19; Purestock/Getty Images, p. 11; samxmeg/E+/Getty Images (moon folios and series logo); Stephanie De Sakutin/AFP/Getty Images, p. 23; Tier Images/Gallo Images/Getty Images, p. 15.

Cover Credits: Pavlo Burdyak/Shutterstock.com (lion); narvikk/E+/Getty Images (starry background); kimberrywood/Digital Vision Vectors/Getty Images (green moon dingbat); samxmeg/E+/Getty Images (moon).